Red Books *showing the way*

LOCAL STREET ATLAS

BATH
BRADFORD-ON-AVON

BATHEASTON · CAMERTON · CORSTON · LARKHALL
PEASEDOWN ST. JOHN · SALTFORD · TIMSBURY · WINSLEY

CONTENTS

LEGEND

—————	...ute
—————	...oad
—————	...d
—————	...ized / Restricted Access
=====	Track
⌐ ⌐	Built Up Area
– – – –	Footpath
~~	Stream
~~	River
~~Lock~~	Canal
——■——	Railway / Station
●	Post Office
P P+	Car Park / Park & Ride
☉	Public Convenience
✚	Place of Worship
→	One-way Street
𝒊	Tourist Information Centre
▲8 ▲8	Adjoining Pages
	Area Depicting Enlarged Centre
	Emergency Services
	Industrial Buildings
	Leisure Buildings
	Education Buildings
	Hotels etc.
	Retail Buildings
	General Buildings
	Woodland
	Orchard
	Recreational / Parkland
	Cemetery

Street plans prepared and published by Red Books (Estate Publications) Ltd, Bridewell House, Tenterden, Kent. The Publishers acknowledge the co-operation of the local authorities of towns represented in this atlas.

Ordnance Survey®   This product includes mapping data licensed from Ordnance Survey® with the permission of the Controller of Her Majesty's Stationery Office.

www.redbooks-maps.co.uk

A B C D

1

Manor Farm
TADWICK LA
KENT LA
BLACKSMITHS LANE
Pickwick Farm
A46
Sch
INNOX

Chilcombe   Bottom

Reservoirs

Upper
Swainswick

ze

2

Weir

GLOUCESTER LANE
SWAINSWICK LANE
BATHEASTON

Little Solsbury
Hill

Fort
Westleigh

Common

LITTLE SOLSBURY LANE
LITTLE SOLSBURY
LANE
LITTLE SOLSBUR

5

LANE
WOOLLEY LANE
LANE

3

Twinfield
Farm

Lam

Brook

Lower
Swainswick

Meadow
Farm

BENNETTS RD
DEADMILL LANE
ROAD
BAILBROOK

Bailbrook
Farm

Bailbrook

Bailbrook
House College

LANE

HIGH
WEST
TOLL BRIDGE RD
WILLOW
MILL

Grange
Farm
Sports
Grnd
Football
Ground

CHARLCOMBE VALLEY

Larkhall

VALLEY
VIEW CL
VIEW
HILL VIEW RD
ROSE HILL
ROAD
ROSE PL
CATSLEY HILL
FERNDALE RD
SWAINSWICK GDNS
GLOUCESTER ROAD
FULLER RD
ORIEL GDNS
GRO
ELM GROVE
THE ELMS

B

4

PICK WICK
WHITE
AVENUE

UPHILL DRIVE
FRYS TERRACE
SPRING VALE
DR
SPRING LA
ELDON TER
EBENT RD
GIFFORDS PL

Recreation
Ground

BROOKLYN RD
DAFFORD
SPA
JESSE
HUGHS
THE
BUTTS
COTTAGE
PL
WOODLA

Nursery

Sports
Field

Weir

Bathampton
Manor

LONDON

ROAD

AVON

BATSTONE CL
COXLEY DR

Schools

BAY

GROSVENOR
LARKHALL PL
Sch
BROMLEAZE
LARKHALL TER
UPPER
LAMBRIDGE MEWS

P

Alice Park

Lambridge
Park

C

5

CHARL-
COMBE
RD
CHARL-
COMBE
RD

5

MALVERN BLDGS
MIDSUMMER
NORF
HAMPTON VW
WORCESTER VILLAS
WORCESTER PL
MAYBOROUGH
WORCESTER TER
VALE PK
SALISBURY PL
WORCESTER ROAD

SPBROUGH
LAMBRIDGE
BRIDGE
HAVORY
SPLAMBRIDGE ST
BEAUFORT WEST

C

RIVER

Kennet & Avon Canal
KENNET
KENNET CT
LANE PK
CANDYS

MILLE
WK

GEORG
CROFT RD
EASTBOURNE AV
TYNING WOOD BLDGS
CLAREMONT
CLAREMONT RD

5

TREE
EASTVILLE
VILLAS
EAST
BOURNE
PK
DOWDING RD
HOLLAND RD
BELGRAVE RD
GROSVENOR VILLAS

Sports
Ground

HAMPTON
HO

BEAUFORT EAST
BEAUFORT PL
GARDENS
GROSVENOR ROAD S
GROSVENOR PK
RINGSWELL

BATHAMPTON

Walkway
PATH
MEADO

DEVONSHIRE
ROAD

RMOND
TER
COBURG
VILLAS
RD
FRANLEY
CHILTON RD
UPPER EAST HAYES
ARUNDEL RD
HIGHBURY

6

ROAD
LONDON

ROAD

MIDDLE EAST HAYES
KENSINGTON PL
GDNS
KENSINGTON
MANVERS
WICK RD

Grosvenor

Grosvenor
Meadows

Grosvenor
Bridge

Avon

WARMINSTER

ROA

BENNETTS LA
Sch
BRUNSWICK ST
LOVE LANE
YORK PL
BURDALLS

Kensington

Superstore

M.O.D.
Government
Offices

ST GEORGES HL
TROSSACHS DR
REGENTS
FIELD
WAY

Pussells

alco
FORESTER RD
WALCOT
CANTON
FORESTER RD
ROCHFORT
CLIFFE
RD
FIELDS
A367

Bath Boating
Station

ROCKCLIFFE
ROCKCLIFFE AV

HAMPTON ROW

WARMINSTER
MINSTER
WAY
MINSTER WAY

Fire
Sta
Amb
FORESTER
AV
FORESTER LA
A36
BATHW

A B C D

10

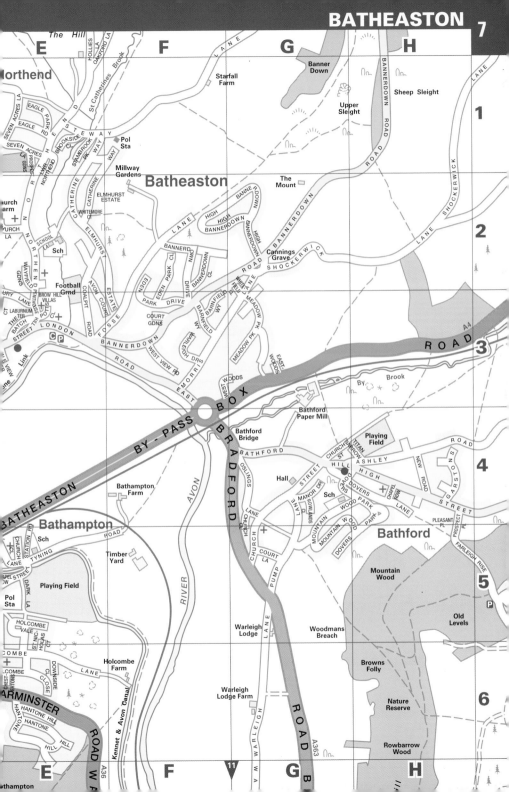

The Hill

Northend

HOLLIES LA
OXFORD LA
St Catherines Brook

Banner Down

Starfall Farm

BANNERDOWN ROAD

Sheep Sleight

SEVEN ACRES LA
EAGLE PARK RD
EAGLE RD
SEVEN ACRES
PROSPECT PL
BROOKSIDE PK
STAMBROOK PK
NORTHEND
STE WAY
WAY
BROOK WAY

Pol Sta

Upper Sleight

1

Millway Gardens

Church Farm
CHURCH LA

Batheaston

The Mount

SHOCKERWICK LANE

ROAD

NORTHEND RD

CATHERINE
CATHERINE
ELMHURST ESTATE
WHITEMORE CT
ELMHURST CT

BANNE R DOWN

HIGH BANNERDOWN

HIGH

2

SCHOOL LA
Sch

BANNERDO
NWN
BANNERDOWN CL

HIGH BANNERDOWN

BANNERDOWN ROAD

Cannings Grave

SHOCKERWICK LANE

WAYFIELD GDNS

EDEN PARK CL
EDEN PARK CL

Football Grnd

AVON COURT
COALPIT ROAD

PARK DRIVE

BARNFIELD WY

DRIVE
BANNERDOWN CL

WHIN LANE
MEADOW PK

MEADOW PK

EAST WOODS

BROW HILL VILLAS
BROW HILL
PENTHOUSE
THE BATCH
LABURNUM CT
STREET
LONDON

COURT GDNS

BARNFIELD

WARLEIGH DRS

BANNERDOWN

WEST VIEW RD

ROAD

EAST

3

WOODS

WOODS

Brook

BY

BATHEASTON

BY - PASS

BOX ROAD

BRADFORD

Bathford Paper Mill

Playing Field

ROAD
A4

ROAD

Bathampton Farm

AVON

Bathford Bridge

BATHFORD

OSLINGS

Hall

Bathford

4

CHURCH ST
TITAN BROW
ASHLEY

HILL

HIGH

STREET

CARSTONS STREET

NEW ROAD

ROAD

Sch

MANOR DR
ROWLANDS
LANE

WOOD PARK

DOVERS

CHAPEL ROW

PLEASANT PL
PROSPECT PL

Bathampton

Sch

ROAD

CHURCH LANE
TYNING

DARK LA

Timber Yard

CHURCH LA

PUMP LANE

COURT LA

MOUNTAIN

MOUNTAIN WOOD

DOVERS

FARLEIGH RISE

Bathford

Mountain Wood

5

CHAPEL STREET
DOWNSIDE CLOSE
HOLCOMBE VALE

Playing Field

Pol Sta

RIVER

Warleigh Lodge

Woodmans Breach

Old Levels

Browns Folly

COMBE
COMBE

Holcombe Farm

LANE

Warleigh Lodge Farm

Nature Reserve

6

WARMINSTER
HANTONE HILL
HANTONE
HANTONE
HILL
HILL

ROAD W

A36

Kennet & Avon Canal

WARLEIGH

ROAD B
A363

Rowbarrow Wood

Bathampton

BATH

E   F   G   H

HILL

Kennet

A36

Rowban Woo

7

A3363

WARLEIGH

BRADFORD

Bathford Hill

1

thampton Wood

Bathampton Wood

RIVER

WARMINSTER

ROAD

Gully Wood

hampton Enclosure

AVON

Kennet & Avon Canal

Warleigh Manor College

Home Wood

Bathford Hill

2

Hengrove Wood

Manor Deer Farm

Manor Farm

ROAD

3

Norwood Playing Fields

Manor Farm

Warleigh

AVENUE

ROAD

Weirs

WARLEIGH

LANE

Claverton Manor (The American Museum)

+

Sheephouse Farm

R.S.P.C.A. Animal Welfare Centre

P

Claverton

Warleigh Hill

4

ERTON

DOWN

LIMEKILN

Vineyards Farm

ROAD

Kennet & Avon Canal

Bassett Farm

ROAD

Link

5

ROAD

Limestone

Warleigh

Wood

WARLEIGH

CLAVERTON

HAZLETON

DR

GDNS FLATS CRES

ERTON RD

DOWN

BRASSKNOCKER

Claverton Wood

Inwood

6

WARMINSTER

WARLEIGH ROAD

Wessex Water H.Q.

asssknocker

HILL

A36

ROAD

15

Dundas

E   F   G   H

Farm

A

Sch

B

8

C

Playing
Field

RL D LL

INNOX GRO

Factory

Englishcombe

Rush   Hill

Wor

1

Breach
Wood

Reservoir

Wansdyke

Hoggen
Coppice

Eastov
Coppie

2

Middle Wood

Vernham
Wood

L A

Woodleaze

3

LANE K I L K E N N Y

ROAD

P+ ▭

KILKENNY

K I L K E N N Y

Down
Wood

ROMAN

Works

L

West
Wood

HAY

4

Duncorn
Hill

Way

COMBE

Fortnight
Farm

ROAD

Week
Wood

Manor House
Farm

Fosse
Farm

5

Westbury
Farm

Week
Farm

B3115

Fosse

TUNLEY

Severcombe
Farm

6

A367

Rainbow
Wood

Limestone   Link

Manc
Fa

Edelweis
Farm

A

B

C

D

A B C D

M.O.D.

Fox Hill

Sports Ground

STONE LA
TRINITY
CLOSE
A 3062
STONE HOUSE
RADLEY RD
WALK

Sp Gro

10

CLAVE DON

Scl

Playing Field

Rec Grnd

BRAMBLE WY
STONE HOUSE CL
FARRS

THE FIRS

CLAVERTON DOWN ROAD

OXFORD PL
GLADSTONE PL
TYNING

SHAFT
PADDOCK WOODS

Combe Grove Manor Hotel

1

NORTH ROAD

Firs Field

AVENUE

WILLIAMS-TOWE

BERKELEY PL
VICTORIA PL

GLADSTONE ROAD

Sports Ground

ST WINIFREDS

Quarry

Golf Course

BRADFORD ROAD
GREEN-DOWN PL
COMBE

WESTERLY RD
QUARRY MANS CT

AVENUE PL
THE

SYDENHAM TER
RICHARDSON PL

OLD CHURCH RD
CHURCH

Sch

DRIVE

Recreation Ground

R O A D

3062

R O A D

HORSECOMBE GRO
SHEPHERDS

HOSPITAL

COMBE CROFT
CME CT

ROAD

THE ORCHARD
THE PADDOCKS

ROCK HALL
PROSPECT PL
BYFIELD
FIELD

CHURCH

BELMONT ROAD

ROAD
MER

Sch

Sch

School

THE BROW

Caves

Quarry

MOUNT PLEASANT

D R U N G W A Y

THE CROFT

SHAFT

Hall

School

2

13

BEECHWOOD

HORSECOMBE VALE

Combe Down

Beach Wood

Horsecombe Vale

Brook

Playing Field

ST MICHAELS
CT

Monkton Combe

CHURCH

MILL LANE

LANE

L A N E

Mill Brook

Midford Brook

Mill Race

We

3

B3110
RO.

MIDFORD

IDFORD ROAD
OLD

MIDFORD ROAD

Pack Horse Farm

Priory Wood

Midford Castle

Weir

Tucking Mill

T U C K I N G

Brett Farm

Short   Wood

4

13

MIDFORD ROAD

ROAD

Limestone   Link

MIDFORD

Weir

Slittems Wood

LANE MIDFORD

Cleeve

Cleeve Rocks

Hayes Wood

Cleeve Farm

5

Cam   Brook

Weir

MIDFORD

M I D F O R D

Brook

Clearbrook Farm

6

Wellow   Brook

H I L L

B3110

PIPEHOUSE

Pipehous

Lower Twinhoe Farm

Hill F

Tumuli

Hog Wood

A B C D

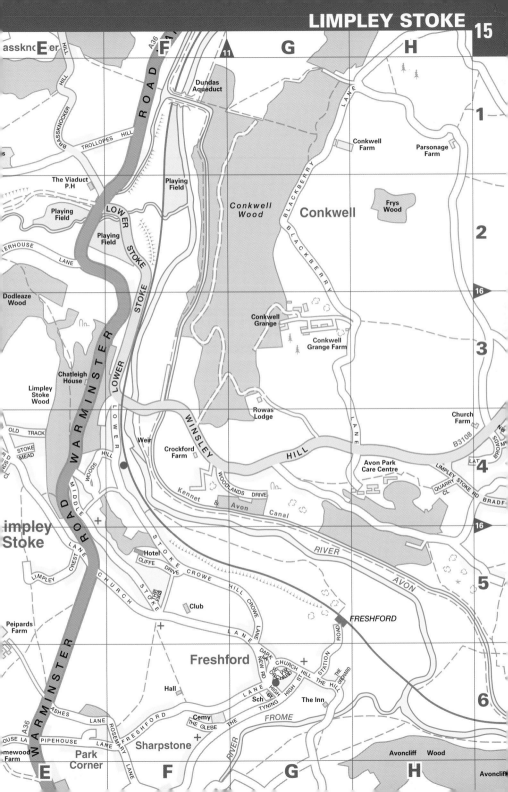

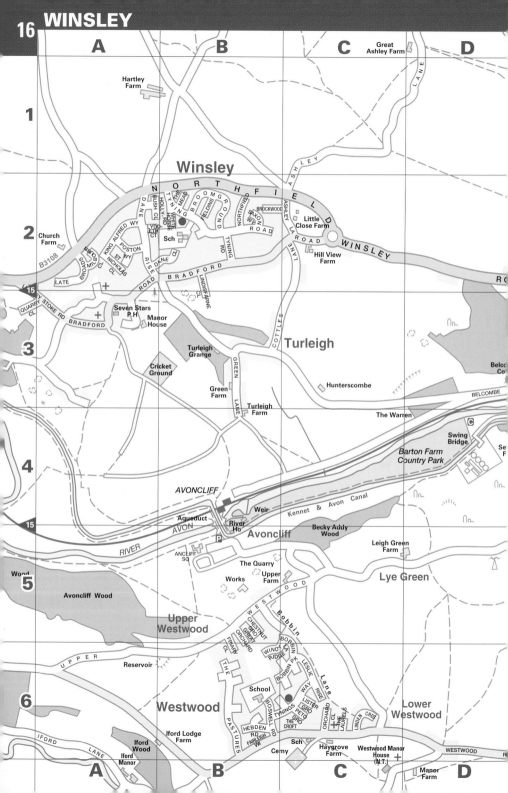

A   B   C   D

Great
Ashley Farm

1

Hartley
Farm

Winsley

N O R T H F I E L D

BROCKWOOD

Little
Close Farm

WINSLEY

ROAD

2

Church
Farm

B3108

BUSH CL
TYNING MEAD
HOLLY RISE
WHITE
SAXON WY
BROOM GROUND
FIELDINS
NORTHFIELD
TYNING
LYDE
LEIGH
CT

Sch

KING ALFRED WY
POSTON WY
NICHOLAS CL
COLUMBUS CL
DANE RISE
DANE

Hill View
Farm

ASHLEY LA ROAD
COTTLES LANE

LATE

BRADFORD
ROAD

LINDISFARNE
CL

15

QUARRY
CL
STOKE RD
BRADFORD

Seven Stars
P.H
Manor
House

Turleigh

Turleigh
Grange

Cricket
Ground

GREEN LANE

Green
Farm

Turleigh
Farm

Hunterscombe

Belco
Co

BELCOMBE

The Warren

Swing
Bridge

Se
F

Barton Farm
Country Park

4

AVONCLIFF

Kennet & Avon Canal

Weir

Aqueduct

AVON

River
Ho

Avoncliff

Becky Addy
Wood

Leigh Green
Farm

ANCLIFF
SQ

P

Lye Green

15

RIVER

The Quarry

Works

Upper
Farm

WESTWOOD

Wood

5

Avoncliff Wood

Upper
Westwood

Bobbin

CHESTNUT
GREAT
ORCHARD
FRIARY
CL

WIND
RIDGE

BOBBIN
BOBBIN PK
LESLIE

BOBBIN
WAY
RISE

LESLIE

Lane

U P P E R

Reservoir

THE

School

BOSWELL RD
TWININGS

LISTER
GRO
PER
THE
CROFT

ORCHARD
THE LAURELS

LINDEN CRES

Lower
Westwood

6

Westwood

PASTURES

HEBDEN
RD
FAIRLEIGH
VW

Sch

Cemy

Haygrove
Farm

Westwood Manor
House
(N.T.)

WESTWOOD

R

IFORD

Iford
Wood

Iford Lodge
Farm

Manor
Farm

LANE

Iford
Manor

A   B   C   D

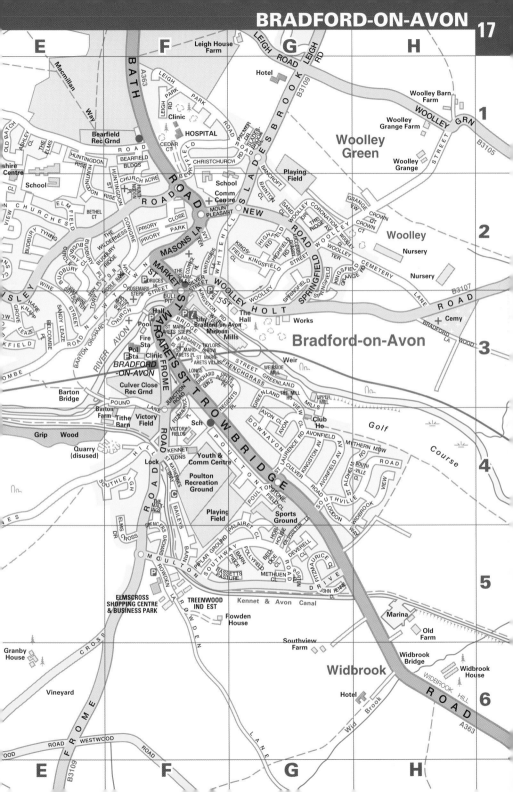

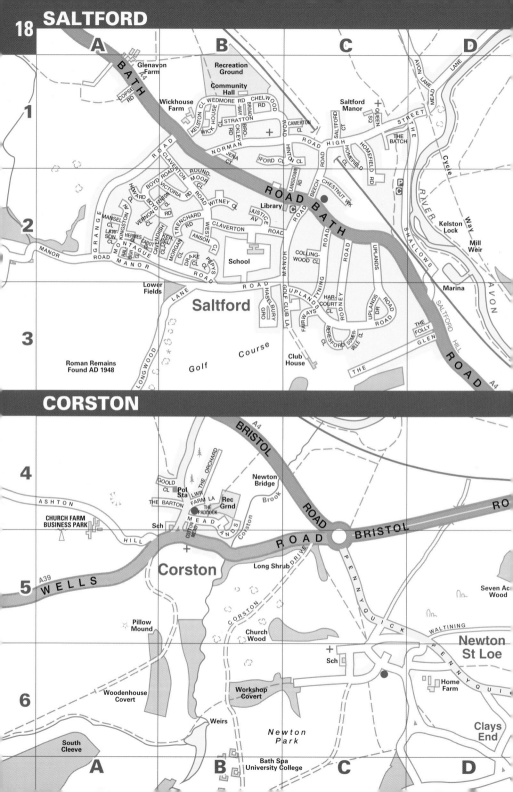

A   **B**   **C**   **D**

1

BATH

COPSE RD

Glenavon Farm

Recreation Ground

Community Hall

Wickhouse Farm

KELSTON CL
WICK HOUSE
WEDMORE RD
CHELWOOD RD
BROAD WAY
STRATTON CL
BECO CL
OXLEY CL
CAMERTON CL
HINTON CL
IFORD CL

NORMAN

JENA CL

Saltford Manor

QUEEN SQ

SALTFORD CT

HIGH

HOMEFIELD RD

STREET THE BATCH

AVON LANE
LANE
MEAD

ROAD

Cycle Way

RIVER

2

MANOR ROAD

ROAD
CLAVERTON ROAD
ROUNDTON RD
HOWARD AV
BOYD RD
VICTORIA RD
MOOR RD
WITNEY CL
MANSEL CL
VERNON CL
BOYD
KINGSTON
BENTON RD
CAVENDISH CL
TRENCHARD RD
WESTON CL
CLAVERTON RD
LAW SON CL
HERMES CL
MONTAGUE
BALL
HIGH CL
CABOT CL
TUCKER CL
MORGAN
DRAKE CL
CL
PEPYS CL
ANSON CL

Library
JUSTICE AV

School

GRANGE

MANOR ROAD

ROAD

ROAD BATH

BEECH

CHESTNUT WK

LANSDOWN RD

COLLINGWOOD CL

ROAD

ROAD

TYNING

UPLANDS

Kelston Lock

SHALLOWS

Mill Weir

Marina

AVON

P C

3

Roman Remains Found AD 1948

LONGWOOD LANE

Lower Fields

Saltford

Golf

Course

HASELBURY GRO

GOLF CLUB LA

UPLANDS

FAIRWAYS

HARCOURT CL

RODNEY

BERESFORD

SOMERVILLE CL

UPLANDS DR

ROAD

THE FOLLY

THE GLEN

Club House

THE

SALTFORD HILL

ROAD A4

4

ASHTON

CHURCH FARM BUSINESS PARK

HILL

GOOLD CL
Pol Sta
THE BARTON
LWR
THE ORCHARD
FARM LA
THE PADDOCK
CORTON MEAD
MEADLANDS
Sch

BRISTOL A4

Newton Bridge

Rec Grnd

Brook

CORSTON

ROAD

BRISTOL

RO

PENNYQUICK

5

A39
WELLS

Corston

Pillow Mound

CORSTON

Long Shrub

DRIVE

Church Wood

Seven Ac Wood

WALTNING

Newton St Loe

PENNYQUICK

6

Woodenhouse Covert

Weirs

Workshop Covert

Newton Park

Sch

Home Farm

Clays End

South Cleeve

Bath Spa University College

A   **B**   **C**   **D**

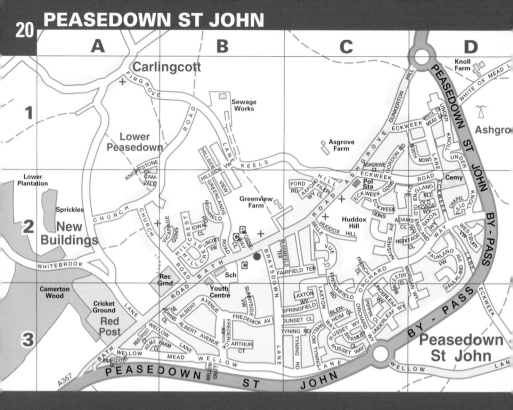

A - Z INDEX TO STREETS
with Postcodes

Blenheim Cl BA2 20 C3
Blenheim Gdns BA1 5 H4
Blind La BA1 4 D4
Bloomfield Av,
Bath BA2 9 F4
Bloomfield Av,
Timsbury BA3 19 B1
Bloomfield Cl BA3 19 B1
Bloomfield Cres BA2 9 F6
Bloomfield Dr BA2 9 E6
Bloomfield Gro BA2 9 F5
Bloomfield Park Rd
BA3 19 B1
Bloomfield Pk BA2 9 F5
Bloomfield Rd,
Bath BA2 9 E6
Bloomfield Rd,
Timsbury BA3 19 B1
Bloomfield Rise BA2 13 E1
Bloomfield Rise North
BA2 9 E6
Bloomfield Ter BA2 20 B2
Boat Stall La BA2 3 C3
Bobbin La BA15 16 B5
Bobbin Pk BA15 16 B6
Boswell Rd BA15 16 B6
Box Rd BA1 7 F4
Boyce Cl BA2 8 A3
Boyd Rd BS31 18 A2
Bradford Pk BA2 13 H1
Bradford Rd,
Bathford BA1 7 F4
Bradford Rd,
Bradford-on-Avon
BA15 16 A3
Bradford Rd,
Combe Down BA2 13 G2
Bradford Wood La
BA15 17 H3
Bramble Way BA2 14 A1
Bramley Cl BA2 20 C3
Brassknocker Hill BA2 11 E6
Brassmill Enterprise
Centre BA1 8 B1
Brassmill La BA1 8 B1
Brassmill Trading
Estate BA1 8 B1
Braysdown Cl BA2 20 A3
Braysdown La BA2 20 B2
Briars Ct BA2 8 B5
Bridewell La BA1 3 B3
Bridge Place Rd BA3 19 E4
Bridge Rd, Bath BA2 9 E4
Bridge Rd,
Grosvenor BA2 6 B6
Bridge St BA2 3 C3
Bridge St*,
Taylors Row BA15 17 F3
Bristol Rd BA2 18 B4
Bristol Vw BA2 13 E2
Broad Quay BA1 3 B5
Broad St BA1 3 B2
Broad Street Pl BA1 3 C2
Broadmoor La BA1 4 B3
Broadmoor Pk BA1 4 C4
Broadmoor Vale BA1 4 C3
Broadway BA2 10 A3
Broadway BS31 18 B1
Brock St BA1 3 A1
Brockley Rd BS31 18 B1
Brockwood BA15 16 B2
Brook Rd BA2 9 E2
Brookfield Pk BA1 4 C4
Brookleaze Bldgs BA1 6 A5
Brooklyn Rd BA1 6 B4
Brookside Cl BA1 7 E1
Brookside Ho BA1 4 C5
Broomground BA15 16 B2
Brougham Hayes BA2 9 F3
Brougham Pl*,
St Saviours St BA1 6 B4
Brow Hill Villas BA1 7 E3
Brunel Ho BA2 8 B2
Brunswick Pl BA1 9 G1
Brunswick St BA1 6 A6
Bruton Av BA2 9 G4
Budbury Circle BA15 17 E2
Budbury Cl BA15 17 E2
Budbury Pl BA15 17 E2
Budbury Ridge BA15 17 E2
Budbury Tyning BA15 17 E2
Bull Pit BA15 17 F3
Bumpers Batch BA2 13 H3
Burdalls Yd BA1 5 H6
Burford Cl BA2 8 C5
Burleigh Gdns BA1 4 C6
Burlington Pl*,
Julian Rd BA1 9 G1
Burlington St BA1 9 G1
Burnham Rd BA2 8 D2
Burnt House Cotts
BA2 13 E2

Burnt House Rd BA2 13 E3
Burton St BA1 3 B3
Byfield BA2 14 A2
Byfield Pl BA2 14 A2
Byron Rd BA2 9 G4

Cabot Cl BS31 18 A2
Cadby Ho BA2 8 B2
Caledonian Rd BA2 9 E3
Calton Gdns BA2 9 G4
Calton Rd BA2 9 H4
Calton Walk BA2 9 H4
Cam Brook Cl BA3 19 E4
Cambridge Pl BA2 10 A3
Cambridge Ter BA2 10 A4
Camden Cres BA1 5 H6
Camden Ct BA1 5 G6
Camden Rd BA1 5 H6
Camden Row BA1 5 H6
Cameley Grn BA2 8 B3
Camerton Cl BS31 18 C1
Camerton Hill BA3 19 E4
Camerton Rd BA3 19 E2
Camvale BA2 20 A2
Canal Ter BA2 7 E5
Canal Vw BA3 19 E4
Canons Cl BA2 8 D6
Canterbury Rd BA2 9 F3
Canton Pl BA1 5 H6
Cardinal Cl BA2 13 E3
Caroline Bldgs*,
Pulteney Rd BA2 10 A3
Caroline Pl BA1 9 H1
Carr Ho BA2 8 B2
Castle Gdns BA2 9 G5
Catherine Pl BA1 9 G1
Catherine Way BA1 7 E2
Catsley Pl BA1 6 B4
Cavendish Cl BS31 18 A2
Cavendish Cres BA1 5 F6
Cavendish Pl BA1 5 G6
Cavendish Rd BA1 5 F6
Cedar Ct BA15 17 F1
Cedar Gro BA2 9 E5
Cedar Villas BA2 9 F3
Cedar Walk BA2 9 F3
Cedar Way BA2 9 F3
Cedric Cl BA1 8 D1
Cedric Rd BA1 4 D6
Cemetery La BA1 17 H2
Chandler Cl BA1 4 C5
Chandos Bldgs BA1 3 B4
Chantry Mead Rd BA2 9 F5
Chapel Ct BA1 3 B4
Chapel Fld BA2 20 D2
Chapel Row, Bath BA1 3 A3
Chapel Row,
Bathampton BA2 7 E5
Chapel Row,
Bathford BA1 7 H4
Charlcombe La BA1 5 G3
Charlcombe Rise BA1 5 G4
Charlcombe View Rd
BA1 5 H4
Charlcombe Way BA1 5 G4
Charles St BA1 3 A3
Charlotte St BA1 9 G2
Charlton Bldgs BA2 9 E2
Charmouth Rd BA1 8 C1
Chatham Pk BA2 10 B2
Chatham Row BA1 9 H1
Chaucer Rd BA2 9 G4
Cheap St BA1 3 C3
Chedworth Cl BA2 11 E6
Chelscombe BA1 4 D5
Chelsea Rd BA1 8 D1
Cheltenham St BA2 9 F3
Chelwood Dr BA2 13 E1
Chelwood Rd BS31 18 B1
Chestnut Gro,
Bath BA2 8 D5
Chestnut Gro,
Bradford-on-Avon
BA15 16 B5
Chestnut Walk BS31 17 F1
Chilton Rd BA1 6 A5
Christchurch Rd BA15 17 F1
Church Acre BA15 17 F2
Church Cl,
Bathampton BA2 7 E5
Church Cl,
Bathford BA1 7 G4
Church Fm
Bsns Pk BA2 18 A4
Church Hill,
Freshford BA3 15 G6
Church Hill,
Timsbury BA3 19 B2
Church La,
Limpley Stoke BA3 15 E5

Church La,
Monkton Combe
BA2 14 D2
Church La,
Northend BA1 7 E2
Church La,
Timsbury BA3 19 B3
Church La,
Widcombe BA2 10 A4
Church Rd,
Combe Down BA2 14 A1
Church Rd,
Weston BA1 4 D5
Church Rd BA2 20 A2
Church St, Bath BA1 3 C4
Church St,
Bathford BA1 7 G5
Church St,
Bradford-on-Avon
BA15 17 F3
Church St,
Weston BA1 4 D5
Church St,
Widcombe BA2 10 A4
Church St,
Woolley BA1 5 G1
Churches BA15 17 E2
Circus Mews BA1 9 G1
Circus Pl BA1 3 B1
City Vw*,
Camden Cres BA1 5 H6
Clare Gdns BA2 13 E2
Claremont Bldgs BA1 5 H5
Claremont Pl*,
Camden Rd BA1 5 H5
Claremont Rd BA1 6 A5
Claremont Walk BA1 5 H5
Clarence Pl BA1 8 D2
Clarence St BA1 5 H6
Clarence Ter BA2 10 C4
Clarendon Rd BA2 10 A4
Clarendon Villas*,
Widcombe Hill BA2 10 A3
Claude Av BA2 9 E4
Claude Ter BA2 9 E4
Claude Vale BA2 9 E4
Claverton Bldgs BA2 3 D6
Claverton Ct BA2 10 C4
Claverton Down Rd
BA2 11 E6
Claverton Dr BA2 11 E6
Claverton Rd BS31 18 B2
Claverton Rd West
BS31 18 B1
Claverton St BA2 3 C6
Cleeve Grn BA2 8 B2
Clevedale Rd BA2 13 H1
Cleveland Cotts BA1 5 H6
Cleveland Ct BA2 10 B2
Cleveland Pl East BA1 5 H6
Cleveland Pl West*,
Cleveland Pl East
BA1 5 H6
Cleveland Reach*,
Cleveland Pl East
BA1 5 H6
Cleveland Walk BA2 10 B2
Cliffe Dr BA3 15 F5
Clyde Gdns BA2 8 C2
Coalpit Rd BA1 7 E2
Coburg Villas BA1 5 H5
Colbourne Rd BA2 13 E2
College Rd BA1 5 F4
College Vw BA1 5 H5
Collier Cl BA3 19 E4
Colliers La BA1 5 G2
Collingwood Cl BS31 18 C2
Combe Gro BA1 8 D1
Combe Hay La BA2 12 C5
Combe Rd BA2 4 D6
Combe Rd BA2 14 A1
Combe Road Cl BA2 14 A1
Combe Royal Cres
BA2 10 C3
Combeside BA2 9 H5
Comfortable Pl*,
Upper Bristol Rd BA2 9 F2
Conigre Hill BA15 17 F2
Connection Rd BA2 8 C2
Conygre Grn BA3 19 B2
Coppice Hill BA15 17 F2
Copse Rd BS31 18 A1
Copseland BA2 10 C4
Cork St BA1 9 E1
Cork Ter BA1 9 E1
Corn St BA1 3 B5
Coronation Av,
Bath BA2 8 D5
Coronation Av,
Bradford-on-Avon
BA15 17 G2

Coronation Cotts*,
High St BA1 7 E3
Coronation Rd BA1 9 E1
Corston Dr BA2 18 B5
Corston Vw BA2 9 E6
Cotswold Rd BA2 9 E4
Cotswold Vw BA2 8 C3
Cottage Pl BA1 6 B4
Cottles La BA15 16 B3
Cotton Mead BA2 18 B5
Court Gdns BA1 7 F3
Court La BA1 7 G5
Cow La BA1 9 F1
Coxley Dr BA1 6 A4
Crandale Rd BA2 9 E3
Cranhill Rd BA1 5 F6
Cranleigh BA2 13 H3
Cranmore Pl BA2 13 F2
Cranwells Pk BA1 5 E6
Cres Vw BA2 9 G3
Crescent Gdns BA1 9 F2
Crescent La BA1 9 G1
Crocombe BA3 19 C2
Crocombe La BA3 19 C1
Croft Rd BA1 6 A5
Crowe Hill BA3 15 F5
Crowe La BA3 15 G5
Crown Cl BA15 17 H2
Crown Hill BA1 4 D5
Crown Rd BA1 4 D5
Culver Rd BA15 17 G4
Cumberland Row BA1 3 A3
Cynthia Rd BA2 9 G3
Cynthia Villas*,
Cynthia Rd BA2 9 E3

Dafford St BA1 6 B4
Daffords Bldgs BA1 6 B4
Daffords Pl*,
Dafford St BA1 6 B4
Dahlia Gdns BA2 10 A1
Daisy Bank BA2 10 A4
Dane Cl BA15 16 A2
Dane Rise BA15 16 A2
Daniel Mews BA2 10 A1
Daniel St BA2 10 A1
Dark La,
Bathampton BA2 7 E5
Dark La,
Freshford BA3 15 G6
Darlington Mews*,
Darlington St BA2 10 A2
Darlington Pl BA2 10 A2
Darlington Rd BA2 10 A1
Darlington St BA2 10 A2
Dartmouth Av BA2 8 D4
Day Cres BA2 8 B2
Deadmill La BA1 6 B4
Deanhill La BA1 4 B4
Denmark Rd BA2 9 E2
Deverell Cl BA15 17 G5
Devonshire Bldgs
BA2 9 G5
Devonshire Mews
BA2 9 G5
Devonshire Pl BA2 9 G5
Devonshire Rd BA2 6 D6
Devonshire Villas BA2 9 G5
Dixon Gdns BA1 5 G6
Dominion Rd BA2 8 C3
Dorcester St BA1 9 H3
Dorchester St BA1 3 C5
Dorset Cl BA2 9 E2
Dorset St BA2 9 E3
Dovers La BA1 7 G4
Dovers Pk BA1 7 G4
Dowding Rd BA1 6 A5
Down Av BA2 13 H1
Down La BA2 6 D5
Downavon BA15 17 G4
Downs Cl BA15 17 E2
Downs Vw BA15 17 E2
Downside Cl BA2 7 E6
Drake Av BA2 9 H6
Drake Cl BS31 18 B2
Dransfield Way BA2 8 D4
Druces Hill BA15 17 F2
Drungway BA2 14 D1
Duke St BA2 3 D4
Duncan Gdns BA1 4 C3
Dunkerton Hill BA2 20 C1
Dunsford Pl BA2 10 A2
Dunster Ho BA2 9 H6
Durcott La BA3 19 C4
Durley Pk BA2 9 F4

Eagle Pk BA1 7 E1
Eagle Rd BA1 7 E1
East Cl BA2 8 C4
East Lea Rd BA1 4 C6
East Way BA2 8 C4
Eastbourne Av BA1 6 A5

Eastbourne Villas*,
Claremont Rd BA1 6 A5
Eastfield Av BA1 4 C4
Eastover Gro BA2 13 E2
Eastville BA1 6 A5
Eastwoods BA1 7 G3
Ebenezer Ter BA2 10 A3
Eckweek Gdns BA2 20 C2
Eckweek La BA2 20 C1
Eckweek Rd BA2 20 C2
Eden Park Cl BA1 7 F3
Eden Park Dr BA1 7 F2
Eden Ter BA1 6 A4
Eden Villas*,
Eden Ter BA1 6 B5
Edgar Bldgs BA1 3 B1
Edgeworth Rd BA2 8 D6
Edward St,
Bathwick BA2 10 A2
Edward St,
Lower Weston BA1 9 E1
Egerton Rd BA2 9 G1
Eldon Pl BA1 6 A4
Eleanor Cl BA2 8 B3
Ellen Ho BA2 8 B3
Elliston Dr BA2 8 B3
Elm Gro,
Englishcombe Park
BA2 9 E5
Elm Gro,
Swainswick BA1 6 B4
Elm Pl BA2 9 G4
Elmfield BA15 17 E2
Elmhurst Est BA1 7 E2
Elms Cross BA15 16 D6
Elms Cross Dr BA15 17 F4
Elmscross
Bsns Pk BA15 17 F5
Elmscross Shopping
Centre BA15 17 F5
Empress Menen Gdns
BA1 4 C6
Englishcombe La BA2 8 C6
Englishcombe Way
BA2 9 F6
Entry Hill BA2 9 G6
Entry Hill Dr BA2 9 G6
Entry Hill Gdns BA2 9 G5
Entry Hill Pk BA2 13 G1
Entry Rise BA2 13 G1
Evelyn Rd BA1 8 C1
Evelyn Ter BA1 5 H5
Excelsior St BA2 10 A3
Exmoor Rd BA2 13 G1

Fairfield Av BA1 5 H4
Fairfield Park Rd BA1 5 H4
Fairfield Rd BA1 6 A5
Fairfield Ter,
Peasedown St John
BA2 20 B2
Fairfield Vw*,
Raglan La BA1 5 H4
Fairleigh Vw BA15 16 B6
Fairways BS31 18 C3
Falconer Rd BA1 4 B3
Farleigh Rise BA1 7 H5
Farleigh Vw*,
Beacon Rd BA1 5 H5
Farrs La BA2 14 A1
Faulkland Rd BA2 9 E4
Faulkland Vw BA2 20 D3
Fenton Cl BS31 18 B2
Ferndale Rd BA1 6 B4
Ferry La BA2 10 A3
Fieldings Rd BA2 8 D2
Fieldins BA15 16 B2
Filer Cl BA2 20 C2
Firgrove La BA2 20 A1
First Av BA2 9 F4
Fitzmaurice Cl BA15 17 G5
Fitzmaurice Pl BA15 17 G5
Flatwoods Cres BA2 11 E6
Flatwoods Rd BA2 11 E6
Follyfield BA15 17 G5
Fonthill Rd BA1 5 F4
Ford Rd BA2 20 C2
Forefield Pl BA2 9 H4
Forefield Rise BA2 10 A4
Forefield Ter BA2 10 A4
Forester Av BA2 10 A1
Forester Ct BA2 6 A6
Forester La BA2 10 A1
Forester Rd BA2 10 A1
Forum Bldgs BA1 3 B5
Fosse Gdns BA2 13 E2
Fosse La BA1 7 E3
Fosseway Cl BA2 20 B2
Fountain Bldgs BA1 3 B1
Fox Hill BA2 9 H6
Foxcombe Rd BA1 8 D1

Frankland Cl BA1 4 C5
Frankley Bldgs BA1 6 A5
Frederick Av BA2 20 B3
Freeview Rd BA2 8 C3
French Cl BA2 20 C2
Frenchfield Rd BA2 20 C2
Frenchgrass BA15 17 F3
Freshford La BA3 15 F6
Friary Cl BA15 16 B5
Frome Rd, Bath BA2 13 E1
Frome Rd,
Bradford-on-Avon
BA15 17 F3
Frys Leaze BA1 6 A4
Fuller Rd BA1 6 B4
Fullers Way BA2 13 E2

Gainsborough Gdns BA1 4 D6
Garfield Ter BA1 6 A6
Garrick Rd BA2 8 B4
Garstons BA1 7 H4
Gay Cl BA1 6 D3
Gay St BA1 3 A1
Gays Hill BA1 5 H6
George St, Bath BA1 3 B2
George St,
Bathwick BA2 10 A2
Georges Rd BA1 5 H5
Georgian Vw BA2 8 D6
Gillingham Ter BA1 6 A6
Gladstone Pl BA2 14 B1
Gladstone Rd BA2 14 B1
Glebe Rd BA2 8 C4
Glencairn Ct BA2 10 A2
Gloster Villas*,
London BA1 9 H1
Gloucester Rd BA1 6 B2
Gloucester St BA1 9 G1
Golf Club La BS31 18 B3
Golf Course Rd BA2 10 B2
Goold Cl BA2 18 B4
Gordon Rd, Bath BA2 10 A4
Gordon Rd,
Peasedown St John
BA2 20 C2
Grand Par BA2 3 C3
Grange Rd BS31 18 B2
Grange Vw BA15 17 G2
Granville Rd BA1 5 F3
Gravel Walk BA1 3 A1
Great Bedford St BA1 5 G6
Great Orchard BA15 16 B5
Great Pulteney St BA2 3 D2
Great Stanhope St
BA1 9 H2
Green La BA15 16 B3
Green Park BA1 9 G3
Green Park Ho BA1 3 A4
Green Park Mews*,
Green Pk BA2 9 G3
Green Park Rd BA1 9 G2
Green St BA1 3 B2
Greenacres BA2 4 C3
Greenbank Gdns BA1 4 C3
Greendown Pl BA2 14 A1
Greenland Mills
BA15 17 G3
Greenland Vw BA15 17 G3
Greenlands Rd BA2 20 B2
Greenvale Cl BA3 19 B3
Greenvale Dr BA3 19 B3
Greenway Ct BA2 9 G5
Greenway La BA2 9 G5
Gregorys Gro BA2 13 E3
Griffin Ct BA1 3 A4
Grosvenor Bridge Rd
BA1 6 B5
Grosvenor Pl BA1 6 B5
Grosvenor Pl BA1 6 A6
Grosvenor Ter BA1 6 B5
Grosvenor Villas BA1 6 A5
Grove Leaze BA15 17 E3
Grove St BA2 3 C1
Guinea La BA1 9 H1

Hadley Rd BA2 10 A6
Hamilton Rd BA1 5 F5
Hampton Ho BA1 6 B5
Hampton Row BA2 6 A6
Hampton Vw BA1 6 A6
Hanna Cl BA2 8 C3
Hanover St BA1 6 A6
Hanover Ter*,
Snow Hill BA1 6 A6
Hansford Cl BA2 13 G2
Hansford Mews BA2 13 G1
Hansford Sq BA2 13 G1
Hantone Hill BA2 7 E6
Harbutts BA2 6 D5
Harcourt Cl BS31 18 C3
Harcourt Gdns BA1 4 D5

Hare Knapp BA15 17 E3
Harley St BA1 9 G1
Harrington Pl BA1 3 B3
Haselbury Gro BS31 18 B3
Hatfield Bldgs BA2 10 A3
Hatfield Rd BA2 9 G5
Haviland Gro BA1 4 C4
Haviland Pk BA1 4 C4
Havory BA1 6 A5
Hawarden Ter BA1 6 A5
Hawthorn Gro BA2 13 G1
Hawthorne Mews
BA2 3 D1
Hay Hill BA1 3 B1
Haycombe Dr BA2 8 B4
Haycombe La BA2 8 A5
Hayden Cl BA2 9 G4
Hayes Pl BA2 9 G4
Hayesfield Pk BA2 9 G4
Hayeswood Rd BA3 19 A2
Haygarth Ct*,
Lansdown Gro BA1 5 G6
Hazel Gro BA2 9 E5
Hazel Way BA2 13 F3
Hazleton Gdns BA1 11 E6
Heather Dr BA2 13 E3
Heathfield Cl BA1 4 C4
Hebden Rd BA15 16 B6
Henrietta Ct BA2 10 A1
Henrietta Gdns BA2 3 D1
Henrietta Mews BA2 3 D2
Henrietta Pl BA2 3 C1
Henrietta Rd BA2 3 D1
Henrietta St BA2 3 D1
Henrietta Villas BA2 3 D1
Henry St BA1 3 C5
Hensley Gdns BA2 9 F5
Hensley Rd BA2 9 F5
Herbert Rd BA2 9 E4
Heritage Cl BA2 20 C2
Hermes Cl BS31 18 A2
Hermitage Rd BA1 5 G5
Hetling Ct BA1 3 B4
High Bannerdown BA1 7 F2
High St, Bath BA1 3 C3
High St,
Bathampton BA2 7 E5
High St,
Batheaston BA1 6 D3
High St, Bathford BA1 7 H4
High St, Bristol BS31 18 C1
High St,
Freshford BA3 15 G6
High St,
Timsbury BA3 19 B2
High St, Twerton BA2 8 D5
High St, Weston BA1 4 C5
High St, Woolley BA1 5 G1
Highbury BA1 5 H6
Highbury Ter BA1 5 H5
Highfield Cl BA2 8 D3
Highfield Rd,
Bath BA2 20 B2
Highfield Rd,
Bradford-on-Avon
BA15 17 G2
Highland Rd BA2 8 C3
Highland Ter BA2 9 E3
Highview BA2 13 G2
Hill Av BA2 13 G2
Hill View BA3 19 B3
Hill View Rd BA1 6 A4
Hillcrest BA2 20 B2
Hillcrest Dr BA2 8 D5
Hillside Rd BA2 9 E4
Hillside Vw BA2 20 B2
Hinton Cl, Bath BA2 8 B2
Hinton Cl,
Bristol BS31 18 C1
Hiscocks Dr BA2 9 F4
Hobhouse Cl BA15 17 G5
Hockley Ct BA1 5 E5
Hodshill BA2 13 G4
Holcombe Cl BA2 7 E6
Holcombe Grn BA1 4 D4
Holcombe La BA2 7 E6
Holcombe Ter BA1 4 D4
Holcombe Vale BA2 7 E5
Holland Rd BA1 6 A5
Hollies La BA1 7 E1
Holloway BA2 3 B6
Holly Dr BA2 13 E3
Holly Pl BA2 8 D5
Hollybush Cl BA15 16 B2
Holt Rd BA15 17 G3
Home Farm La BA2 20 A3
Homefield BA3 19 C2
Homefield Cl BS31 18 C1
Homefield Rd BS31 18 C1
Homelea Pk East BA1 8 B1
Homelea Pk West BA1 8 B1
Hook Hill BA3 19 D2

Horsecombe Brow
BA2 13 H2
Horsecombe Gro
BA2 13 H1
Horsecombe Vale
BA2 13 H2
Horseshoe Rd BA3 10 B3
Horseshoe Walk BA2 10 A3
Horton Cl BA15 17 G5
Hortsmann Cl BA1 8 D1
Hot Bath St BA1 3 B4
How Hill BA2 8 C2
Howard Cl BS31 18 A2
Huddox Hill BA2 20 C2
Hungerford Rd BA1 9 E1
Huntingdon Pl BA15 17 F2
Huntingdon Rise
BA15 17 E1
Huntingdon St BA15 17 F1

Idwal Cl BA2 20 B2
Iford Cl BS31 18 B1
Iford La BA15 16 A6
Innox Gro BA2 12 B1
Innox La BA1 6 A1
Innox Rd BA2 8 D3
Inverness Rd BA2 8 D2
Ivo Peters Rd BA2 9 F2
Ivy Av BA2 8 D5
Ivy Bank Pk BA2 9 G6
Ivy Cotts BA2 13 G4
Ivy Gro BA2 8 D4
Ivy Pl BA2 8 D4
Ivy Ter BA15 17 F2
Ivy Villas BA2 8 D4

James St West BA1 3 A4
Jena Ct BA2 8 D5
Jesse Hughes Ct BA1 6 B4
Jews La BA2 8 D3
John Rennie Cl BA15 17 G5
John St BA1 3 B2
Johnstone St BA2 3 D2
Jones Hill BA15 17 E5
Julian Rd BA1 9 G1
Junction Av BA2 9 F4
Junction Rd, Bath BA2 9 F3
Junction Rd,
Bradford-on-Avon
BA15 17 F3
Justice Av BS31 18 B2

Kaynton Mead BA1 8 D2
Keels Hill BA2 20 B1
Kelso Rd BA2 9 E1
Kelston Cl BS31 18 B1
Kelston Rd BA1 4 A5
Kelston Vw BA2 8 B4
Kenilworth Ct*,
Snow Hill BA1 6 A5
Kennet Cl BA2 6 D5
Kennet Gdns BA15 17 F4
Kennet Pk BA2 6 D5
Kennington Rd BA1 8 D1
Kensington Ct BA1 6 A6
Kensington Gdns BA1 6 A6
Kensington Pl BA1 6 A6
Kent La BA1 6 A1
Keppel Cl BS31 18 B2
Kewstoke Rd BA2 13 H1
Kilkenny La BA2 12 A3
Kinber Cl BA1 4 B3
King Alfred Way
BA15 16 A2
King Edward Rd BA2 9 F4
King Georges Rd BA2 8 D3
Kingsdown Vw BA1 5 H5
Kingsfield, Bath BA2 8 D6
Kingsfield,
Bradford-on-Avon
BA15 17 G2
Kingsfield Cl BA15 17 G2
Kingsfield Grange Rd
BA15 17 G2
Kingsmead Ct BA1 3 A4
Kingsmead East BA1 3 A4
Kingsmead North BA1 3 A4
Kingsmead Sq BA1 3 A4
Kingsmead St BA1 3 A3
Kingsmead Ter BA1 3 A4
Kingsmead West BA1 3 A4
Kingston Av,
Bradford-on-Avon
BA15 17 G4
Kingston Av,
Bristol BS31 18 A2
Kingston Bldgs BA1 3 C4
Kingston Par BA1 3 C4
Kingston Rd, Bath BA1 3 C5
Kingston Rd,
Bradford-on-Avon
BA15 17 F3

Kingsway BA2 8 D5
Kipling Av BA2 9 G4
Knightstone Cl BA2 20 A2
Knightstone Pl BA1 4 C5
Kyrle Gdns BA1 6 D3

Laburnum Ter BA1 7 E3
Laggan Gdns BA1 5 H5
Lambridge Mews BA1 6 B5
Lambridge Pl BA1 6 B5
Lambridge St BA1 6 B5
Lampards Bldgs*,
Balance St BA1 9 G1
Landseer Rd BA2 8 C3
Langdon Rd BA2 8 C4
Lansdown Cres,
Bath BA1 5 G6
Lansdown Cres,
Timsbury BA3 19 C2
Lansdown Gro BA1 5 G6
Lansdown Heights
BA1 5 G5
Lansdown La BA1 4 C3
Lansdown Mansions*,
Lansdown Rd BA1 5 G6
Lansdown Mews BA1 3 B1
Lansdown Pk BA1 5 F4
Lansdown Pl East
BA1 5 G6
Lansdown Pl West
BA1 5 G6
Lansdown Rd,
Bath BA1 3 B1
Lansdown Rd,
Bristol BS31 18 C2
Lansdown Ter BA1 4 D5
Lansdown Ter*,
Timsbury BA3 19 C2
Lansdown Vw,
Twerton BA2 8 D3
Lansdown Vw,
Larkhall BA1 6 B5
Larkhall Pl BA1 6 B5
Larkhall Ter BA1 6 B5
Late Broads BA15 16 A2
Laura Pl BA2 3 D2
Laurel Gdns BA3 19 B3
Lawson Cl BS31 18 A2
Laxton Way BA2 20 C3
Leigh Cl BA1 5 H5
Leigh Park Rd BA15 17 F1
Leighton Rd BA1 4 B3
Leopold Bldgs*,
Upper Hedgemead Rd
BA1 5 H6
Leslie Rise BA15 16 C6
Lilliput Ct BA1 3 C4
Lime Gro BA2 10 A3
Lime Grove Gdns
BA2 10 A3
Limekiln La BA2 11 E5
Limpley Crest BA15 15 E5
Limpley Stoke Rd
BA15 15 H4
Lincott Vw BA2 20 B2
Linden Cres BA15 16 C6
Linden Gdns BA1 5 E6
Lindisfarne Cl BA15 16 B2
Linley Cl BA2 8 B3
Lime Ho BA2 8 B3
Lippiatt La BA3 19 C2
Lister Gro BA15 16 C6
Little Hill BA2 8 C2
Little Solsbury La BA1 6 C2
Little Stanhope St BA1 9 G2
Livingstone Rd BA2 9 E3
Livingstone Ter*,
Junction Rd BA2 9 F3
Locksbrook Rd BA1 8 C2
**Locksbrook
Trading Est BA1 8 D2**
Loddon Way BA15 17 G4
Lodge Gdns BA2 13 E1
London Rd BA1 5 H6
London Rd East BA1 7 E3
London Rd West BA1 6 C4
Long Acre BA1 5 H6
Long Hay Cl BA2 8 D3
Long Valley Rd BA2 8 A3
Longfellow Av BA2 9 G5
Longs Yd BA15 17 G2
Longwood La BS31 18 A3
Lorne Rd BA2 9 E3
Loves Hill BA3 19 A3
Lower Borough Walls
BA1 3 B4
Lower Bristol Rd BA2 3 A5
Lower Camden Pl*,
Upper Camden Rd
BA1 5 H6
Lower East Hayes BA1 6 A6

Lower Farm La BA2 18 B4
Lower Hedgemead Rd
BA1 5 H6
Lower Northend BA1 7 E1
Lower Oldfield Pk BA2 9 F3
Lower Stoke BA2 15 F2
Loxley Gdns BA2 8 D4
Loxton Dr BA2 8 D3
Luccombe Quarry
BA15 17 G2
Lucklands Rd BA1 4 D5
Lyddieth Ct BA15 16 A2
Lyme Gdns BA1 8 C1
Lyme Rd BA1 8 C1
Lymore Av BA2 8 D3
Lymore Gdns BA2 9 E4
Lympsham Grn BA2 13 F2
Lynbrook La BA2 9 G6
Lyncombe Hill BA2 3 D6
Lyncombe Vale BA2 10 A5
Lyncombe Vale Rd
BA2 9 H5
Lyndhurst Pl*,
Thomas St BA1 5 H6
Lyndhurst Rd BA2 9 E3
Lyndhurst Ter BA1 5 H6
Lynfield Pk BA1 4 C5
Lytton Gdns BA2 8 C5

Macaulay Bldgs BA2 10 B4
Magdalen Av BA2 3 A6
Magdalen Rd BA2 3 A6
Maggs Hill BA3 19 C2
Magnon Rd BA15 17 E2
Malvern Bldgs BA1 5 H5
Malvern Ter BA1 5 H6
Malvern Villas*,
Camden Rd BA1 5 H6
Manor Dr BA1 7 G4
Manor Pk BA1 4 C6
Manor Rd, Bath BA1 4 D5
Manor Rd,
Bristol BS31 18 A2
Manor Villas*,
Weston Pk BA1 4 D5
Mansel Cl BS31 18 A2
Manvers St BA1 3 D5
Maple Gdns BA2 9 F4
Maple Gro BA2 9 F4
Marchants Pass BA1 3 C5
Margarets Bldgs BA1 3 A1
Margarets Hill BA1 5 H6
Market St BA15 17 F2
Marlborough Bldgs
BA1 9 F1
Marlborough La BA1 9 F1
Marlbourgh St BA1 9 G1
Marsden Rd BA2 8 D6
Marshfield Way BA1 5 H5
Masons La BA15 17 F2
Maybrick Rd BA2 9 E3
Mayfield Rd BA2 9 E3
Mead Cl BA2 9 F5
Mead La BS31 18 D1
Meade Ho BA2 8 B3
Meadlands BA2 18 B4
Meadow Dr BA2 13 F3
Meadow Gdns BA1 4 C6
Meadow La BA2 6 C6
Meadow Pk BA1 7 G3
Meadow View Cl BA1 4 B6
Meadowfield BA15 16 D3
Meare Rd BA2 9 H6
Melcombe Ct BA2 9 E4
Melcombe Rd BA2 9 E4
Melrose Gro BA2 8 D5
Melrose Ter*,
Raglan La BA1 5 H5
Memorial Cotts*,
Weston Pk BA1 4 D6
Mendip Gdns BA2 13 E2
Methuen Cl BA15 17 G5
Michaels Mead BA1 4 C4
Middle La BA1 6 A6
Middle Rank BA15 17 F3
Middle Stoke BA3 15 E4
Midford Hill BA2 14 B5
Midford Rd BA2 13 F1
Midland Bridge Rd
BA2 9 F3
Midland Rd BA2 9 F2
Midsummer Bldgs
BA1 6 A5
Milburn Cl BA15 16 A2
Miles St BA2 10 A3
Miles's Bldgs BA1 9 G1
Milk St BA1 3 A5
Mill La,
Bathampton BA2 6 D4

Mill La, Bradford-on-Avon BA15 17 F3
Mill La, Monkton Combe BA2 14 D2
Mill La, Timsbury BA3 19 B3
Mill La, Twerton BA2 8 C3
Millbrook Pl BA2 10 A4
Miller Walk BA2 6 D5
Millmead Rd BA2 9 E3
Milsom St BA1 3 B2
Milton Av BA2 9 G4
Minerva Gdns BA2 8 D4
Minster Way BA2 10 B1
Monksdale Rd BA2 9 E5
Monmouth Pl BA1 9 G2
Monmouth St BA1 3 A3
Montague Rd BS31 18 A2
Montpelier BA1 9 G1
Montrose Cotts BA1 4 D6
Moorfields Cl BA2 9 E5
Moorfields Rd BA2 9 E5
Moorland Rd BA2 9 E3
Morford St BA1 9 G1
Morgan Cl BS31 18 B2
Morgan Way BA2 20 C2
Morley Ter BA2 9 E2
Morris La BA1 7 F3
Mortimer Cl BA1 4 D4
Moulton Dr BA15 17 F5
Mount Beacon BA1 5 H6
Mount Beacon Pl BA1 5 H6
Mount Beacon Row*, Beacon Rd BA1 5 H5
Mount Gro BA2 8 C6
Mount Pleasant, Bath BA2 14 C2
Mount Pleasant, Bradford-on-Avon BA15 17 F2
Mount Rd, Lansdown BA1 5 H6
Mount Rd, Southdown BA2 8 C4
Mount Vw BA2 8 C5
Mount Vw*, Beacon Rd BA1 5 H5
Mountain Ash BA1 5 E5
Mountain Wood BA1 7 G5
Mythern Mdw BA15 17 G4

Naishes Av BA2 20 C2
Napier Rd BA1 4 B3
Nelson Pl East*, Nelson Ter BA1 5 H6
Nelson Pl West BA1 9 F2
Nelson Ter BA1 5 H6
Nelson Villas, Bath BA1 9 F2
Nelson Villas, Weston BA1 4 C5
New Bond St BA1 3 B3
New Bond Street Bldgs BA1 3 B3
New Bond Street Pl BA1 3 C3
New King St BA1 3 A3
New Orchard St BA1 3 C5
New Rd, Bathford BA1 7 H4
New Rd, Bradford-on-Avon BA15 17 G2
New Rd, Freshford BA3 15 G6
New St BA1 3 A4
New Tyning Ter*, Fairfield Rd BA1 6 A5
Newark St BA1 3 C5
Newbridge Ct BA1 8 D1
Newbridge Gdns BA1 8 B1
Newbridge Hill BA1 8 C1
Newbridge Rd BA1 4 A6
Newmans La BA3 19 B2
Newmarket Row*, Grand Par BA2 3 C3
Newton Rd BA2 8 A3
Newtown BA15 17 E3
Nile St BA1 9 G2
Norfolk Bldgs BA1 9 G2
Norfolk Cres BA1 9 F2
Norfolk Ter*, Lower Bristol Rd BA2 9 F2
Norman Rd BS31 18 B1
North La BA2 10 C3
North Mdws BA2 20 D1
North Par BA1 3 D4
North Parade Bldgs BA1 3 C4
North Parade Bri BA2 3 D4
North Parade Pass BA1 3 C4
North Parade Rd BA2 3 D4
North Rd, Bathwick BA2 10 B1
North Rd, Combe Down BA2 14 A1
North Rd, Timsbury BA3 19 B2
North View Cl BA2 8 C4
North Way BA2 8 B4
Northampton Bldgs BA1 9 G1
Northampton St BA1 9 G1
Northend BA1 7 E2
Northfield BA15 16 A2
Northfields BA1 5 G5
Northfields Cl BA1 5 G5
Northgate St BA1 3 C2
Northumberland Pl BA1 3 C3
Norwood Av BA2 10 D4

Oak Av BA2 9 E5
Oak St BA2 3 A6
Oakfield Cl BA1 9 E1
Oakford La BA1 7 E1
Oakhill Rd BA2 13 G1
Oakley BA2 10 C4
Odins Rd BA2 13 E1
Old Bond St BA1 3 B3
Old Church Ct BA2 14 B1
Old England Way BA2 20 D2
Old Ferry Rd*, Lower Bristol Rd BA2 8 D2
Old Forge Way BA2 20 D2
Old Fosse Rd BA2 13 E1
Old Frome Rd BA2 13 G2
Old King St BA1 3 B2
Old Midford Rd BA2 13 H3
Old Newbridge Hill BA1 4 B6
Old Orchard BA1 3 C1
Old Orchard St BA1 3 C4
Old Quarry BA2 9 E6
Old Track BA3 15 E4
Oldfield La BA2 9 E4
Oldfield Pl BA2 9 F3
Oldfield Rd BA2 9 F4
Onega Ter BA1 9 F2
Oolite Gro BA2 13 E2
Oolite Rd BA2 13 E1
Orange Gro BA1 3 C3
Orchard Cl BA15 16 C6
Orchard Gdns BA15 17 F3
Orchard Ter BA2 8 C3
Orchard Way BA2 20 C3
Oriel Gdns BA1 6 B4
Oriel Gro BA2 8 D5
Osborne Rd BA1 8 C2
Oslings La BA1 7 G4
Otago Ter BA1 6 B4
Overdale BA3 19 F2
Oxford Pl BA2 14 B1
Oxford Row BA1 3 B1
Oxford Ter BA2 14 B1
Oxney Pl*, Braysdown La BA2 20 B2

Pack Horse La BA2 13 G3
Paddock Woods BA2 10 C6
Padfield Cl BA2 8 D4
Padleigh Hill BA2 8 C6
Palace Yard Mews BA1 3 A2
Palairet Cl BA15 17 G5
Palmer Dr BA15 17 G1
Paragon BA1 3 B1
Park Av BA2 9 G4
Park Gdns BA1 9 E1
Park La BA1 9 E1
Park Pl BA1 5 G6
Park Rd BA1 8 D1
Park St BA1 5 G6
Park St Mews BA1 5 G6
Parkway BA3 19 E2
Parkway La BA3 19 D1
Parry Cl BA2 8 D4
Parsonage La BA1 3 B3
Partis Way BA1 4 C6
Peasedown St John By-Pass BA2 20 A3
Pembroke Ct BA1 4 D5
Penn Gdns BA1 4 B6
Penn Hill Rd BA1 4 B6
Penn Lea Ct BA1 8 C1
Penn Lea Rd BA1 4 C6
Pennard Grn BA2 8 B3
Pennyquick BA2 18 C5
Pennyquick Vw BA2 8 A2
Penthouse Hill BA1 7 E2
Pepys Cl BS31 18 B2
Pera Pl BA1 5 H6
Pera Rd BA1 5 H6
Percy Pl BA1 6 A6
Perfect Vw BA1 5 H5
Peto Gro BA15 16 C6
Philip St BA1 3 C5
Piccadilly Pl BA1 6 A6
Pickwick Rd BA1 5 H4
Pierrepont Pl BA1 3 C4
Pierrepont St BA1 3 D4
Pine Way Ind Est*, Pines Way BA2 9 F2
Pines Way BA2 9 F2
Pioneer Av BA2 13 H1
Pipehouse La BA3 15 E6
Piplar Ground BA15 17 F5
Pippin Cl BA2 20 C3
Pitman Ct BA1 6 B4
Pleasant Pl BA1 7 H4
Podgers Dr BA1 4 D4
Poole Ho BA2 8 B3
Poolmead Rd BA2 8 B4
Popes Walk BA2 10 A5
Poplar Cl BA2 9 E4
Poplar Rd BA2 13 E3
Portland Pl BA1 9 G1
Portland Ter*, Harley St BA1 9 G1
Poston Way BA15 16 A2
Potts Cl BA1 7 E3
Poulton BA15 17 F4
Poulton La BA15 17 G5
Pound La BA15 17 F3
Powlett Ct BA2 10 A1
Powlett Rd BA2 10 A1
Priddy Cl BA2 8 D3
Primrose Hill BA1 5 E5
Princes Bldgs*, Pulteney Rd BA2 10 A3
Princes St BA1 3 A3
Prior Park Cotts BA2 10 A4
Prior Park Gdns BA2 10 A4
Prior Park Rd BA2 10 A4
Priors Hill BA3 19 A3
Priory Cl, Bath BA2 10 A6
Priory Cl, Bradford-on-Avon BA15 17 F2
Priory Pk BA15 17 F2
Prospect Gdns BA1 7 E1
Prospect Pl, Bathford BA1 7 H5
Prospect Pl, Beacon Hill BA1 5 H6
Prospect Pl, Combe Down BA2 14 A2
Prospect Pl, Oldfield Park BA2 9 G4
Prospect Pl, Weston BA1 4 D4
Prospect Rd BA2 10 B4
Pulteney Av BA2 10 A3
Pulteney Bri BA2 3 C3
Pulteney Gdns BA2 10 A3
Pulteney Gro BA2 10 A3
Pulteney Mews BA2 3 D2
Pulteney Rd BA2 10 A2
Pulteney Ter*, Pulteney Rd BA2 10 A3
Pump La BA1 7 G5
Purlewent Dr BA1 4 D5
Purlock Rd BA2 13 H1

Quantocks BA2 13 H1
Quarry Cl, Bath BA2 13 G1
Quarry Cl, Bradford-on-Avon BA15 15 H4
Quarry Rd BA2 10 C3
Quarrymans Ct BA2 14 A1
Quebec BA2 8 C3
Queen Sq, Bath BA1 3 A2
Queen Sq, Bristol BS31 18 C1
Queen Square Pl BA1 9 G2
Queen St BA1 3 B3
Queens Dr BA2 9 H6
Queens Par BA1 9 G2
Queens Parade Pl BA1 3 A2
Queens Pl BA2 10 A3
Queenwood Av BA1 5 H5
Quiet St BA1 3 B2

Raby Mews BA2 10 A2
Raby Pl BA2 10 A2
Raby Villas BA2 10 A2
Rackfield Pl BA2 8 D2
Radford Hill BA3 19 C3
Raglan Cl*, Raglan La BA1 5 H5
Raglan La BA1 5 H5
Raglan St BA1 5 H5
Raglan Ter BA1 5 H5
Raglan Villas BA1 5 H5
Railway Pl BA1 3 D6
Railway St BA1 3 C5
Raleigh Cl BS31 18 A2
Ralph Allen Dr BA2 10 A5
Rectory La BA3 19 C2
Red Hill BA3 19 E4
Red Post Ct BA2 20 A3
Redland Pk BA2 8 B2
Regents Fld BA2 6 C6
Regents Pl BA15 17 F4
Richardson Pl BA2 14 B1
Richmond Cl BA1 5 H5
Richmond Heights BA1 5 G5
Richmond Hill BA1 5 G6
Richmond La BA1 5 H6
Richmond Pl BA1 5 G5
Richmond Rd BA1 5 G4
Richmond Ter BA1 5 H5
Rickfield BA15 17 E3
Ridge Green Cl BA2 13 F3
Ringswell Gdns BA1 6 B6
Ringwood Rd BA2 9 E3
River Pl BA2 8 D2
Rivers Rd BA1 5 H6
Rivers St BA1 9 G1
Rivers Street Mews BA1 9 G1
Rivers Street Pl*, Rivers St BA1 9 G1
Riverside Ct BA2 3 C1
Riverside Ct*, Riverside Rd BA2 9 G3
Riverside Gdns BA1 3 A5
Riverside Rd BA2 9 G3
Riverside Ter BA1 3 C2
Rochfort Ct BA2 6 A6
Rochfort Pl BA2 10 A1
Rock Hall La BA2 14 A1
Rock La BA2 14 A1
Rockcliffe Av BA2 6 A6
Rockcliffe Rd BA2 6 A6
Rodney Ho BA2 8 B2
Rodney Rd BS31 18 C3
Rooksbridge Walk BA2 8 D3
Rose Cotts BA2 13 G4
Rose Hill BA1 6 A4
Roseberry Rd BA2 9 E2
Roseland Cl BA1 6 B4
Rosemary La BA3 15 F6
Rosemary Steps BA15 17 F2
Rosemary Walk BA15 17 F3
Rosemount La BA2 10 A4
Rosewarn Cl BA2 8 B4
Rosewell Ct BA1 3 A3
Rossiter Rd BA2 3 D6
Rosslyn Cl BA1 8 C1
Rosslyn Rd BA1 8 C2
Roundhill Gro BA2 8 C5
Roundhill Pk BA2 8 C5
Roundmoor Cl BS31 18 B2
Rowacres BA2 8 C6
Rowden La BA15 17 F5
Rowlands Cl BA1 7 G4
Royal Av BA1 3 A1
Royal Cres BA1 9 F1
Royal Crescent Mews BA1 9 G1
Rudmore Pk BA1 8 C1
Rush Hill BA2 8 C6
Russell St BA1 9 G1
Russet Way BA2 20 C3

St Aldhelm Rd BA15 17 G4
St Andrews Ter BA1 3 B1
St Anns Pl*, Monmouth Pl BA1 9 G2
St Anns Way BA2 10 A2
St Catherines Cl BA2 10 B2
St Christophers Cl BA2 10 B1
St Georges Bldgs*, Upper Bristol Rd BA1 9 F2
St Georges Hill BA2 6 C6
St Georges Pl*, Upper Bristol Rd BA1 9 F2
St James's Par BA1 3 B4
St James's Pk BA1 5 G6
St James's Pl*, St James's Sq BA1 9 G1
St James's Sq BA1 9 G1
St James's St BA1 9 G1
St Johns Cl BA2 20 B3
St Johns Pl BA1 3 B3
St Johns Rd, Bath BA2 3 C1
St Johns Rd, Lower Weston BA1 9 E1
St Johns Rd, Timsbury BA3 19 B3
St Katherines Quay BA15 17 F4
St Kildas Rd BA2 9 E4
St Laurence Rd BA15 17 G4
St Lukes Rd BA2 9 G5
St Margarets Hill BA15 17 F3
St Margarets Pl BA15 17 F3
St Margarets St BA15 17 F3
St Margarets Steps BA15 17 F3
St Margarets Villas BA15 17 F3
St Marks Gdns BA2 3 B6
St Marks Rd BA2 3 C6
St Martins Ct BA2 13 F2
St Marys Bldgs BA2 3 A6
St Marys Cl, Bathwick BA2 10 A2
St Marys Cl, Timsbury BA3 19 B2
St Marys Rise BA3 19 B3
St Matthews Pl*, Pulteney Rd BA2 10 A3
St Michaels Ct BA2 14 D2
St Michaels Pl BA1 3 B4
St Michaels Rd, Lower Weston BA1 9 E1
St Michaels Rd, Twerton BA2 8 B4
St Nicholas Cl BA15 16 A2
St Nicholas Ct BA2 7 E6
St Patricks Ct BA2 10 A2
St Pauls Pl BA1 3 A3
St Peters Ter BA2 9 F2
St Saviours Rd BA1 6 A5
St Saviours Ter*, St Saviours Rd BA1 6 A5
St Saviours Way BA1 6 B5
St Stephens Cl BA1 5 G6
St Stephens Ct BA1 5 G6
St Stephens Rd BA1 5 G6
St Swithins Pl BA1 9 H1
St Swithins Yd BA1 9 H1
St Winifreds Dr BA2 14 C1
Salisbury Rd BA1 6 A5
Saltford Ct BS31 18 C1
Saltford Hill BS31 18 D3
Sand Cl BA15 17 G2
Sandy Leaze BA15 17 E3
Saracen St BA1 3 C2
Saville Row BA1 3 B1
Sawclose BA1 3 B3
Saxon Ct BA1 3 B2
Saxon Way, Bath BA2 20 D2
Saxon Way, Bradford-on-Avon BA15 16 B2
School La BA1 7 E2
Second Av BA2 9 F4
Sedgemoor Rd BA2 13 H1
Selbourne Cl BA1 8 B1
Selworthy Ho BA2 9 H6
Seven Acres La BA1 7 E1
Seymour Rd BA1 5 H6
Shaft Rd BA2 14 C1
Shaftesbury Av BA1 8 D2
Shaftesbury Mews*, Beckhampton Rd BA2 9 E4
Shaftesbury Rd BA2 9 F3
Shakespeare Av BA2 9 G4
Sham Castle La BA2 10 A1
Shaws Way BA2 8 A3
Shelley Rd BA2 9 G4
Shepherds Walk BA2 13 G2
Sheridan Rd BA2 8 B4
Shickle Gro BA2 13 E2
Shires Yd BA1 3 B2
Shockerwick La BA1 7 G2
Shophouse Rd BA2 8 D3
Silver St BA15 17 F2
Sion Hill BA1 5 F6
Sion Pl BA2 10 B2
Sion Rd BA1 5 F5
Sladebrook Av BA2 8 D5
Sladebrook Ct BA2 8 D5
Sladebrook Rd BA2 8 C5
Sladesbrook BA15 17 G2
Sladesbrook Cl BA15 17 G1
Snow Hill BA1 5 H6
Solsbury Ct BA1 7 E3
Solsbury La BA1 7 E3
Solsbury Vw*, Raglan La BA1 5 H6
Solsbury Way BA1 5 H4
Somerdale Av BA2 13 E1
Somerset Folly BA3 19 B2
Somerset La BA1 5 F6

Somerset Pl BA1	5 F6
Somerset St BA1	3 B5
Somerville Cl BS31	18 C3
South Av BA2	9 E3
South Gate BA1	9 H3
South Lea Rd BA1	4 C6
South Par BA2	3 D4
South Rd BA3	19 B3
South View Pl BA2	13 E2
South View Rd BA2	9 E2
South Vw BA3	19 C2
South Vw*, Camden Rd BA1	5 H5
Southbourne Gdns BA1	6 A5
Southcot Pl BA2	9 H4
Southdown Av BA2	8 C5
Southdown Rd BA2	8 D5
Southgate BA1	3 C5
Southgate Shopping Centre BA1	**3 C5**
Southlands BA1	4 C5
Southlands Dr BA3	19 B3
Southleigh BA15	17 E4
Southstoke La BA2	13 G3
Southstoke Rd BA2	13 G2
Southville Cl BA15	17 H4
Southville Rd BA15	17 G4
Southville Ter BA2	10 A5
Southway Rd BA15	17 F5
Spa La BA1	6 B4
Spencers Belle Vue BA1	5 G6
Spencers Orchard BA15	17 F5
Spring Cres BA2	10 A3
Spring Gardens Rd, Bath BA2	3 C2
Spring Gardens Rd, Bath BA2	3 D5
Spring La BA1	6 A4
Spring Vale BA1	6 A4
Springfield, Bath BA2	20 C3
Springfield, Bradford-on-Avon BA15	17 G3
Springfield Cl BA2	8 D3
Springfield Pl BA1	5 G5
Spruce Way BA2	13 F3
Stable Yd BA2	9 E2
Stall St BA1	3 C3
Stambrook Pk BA1	7 E1
Stanhope Pl BA1	9 G2
Stanier Rd BA2	9 F2
Stanley Rd West BA2	9 E3
Stanway Cl BA2	13 E1
Station Rd, Bathampton BA2	7 E5
Station Rd, Freshford BA3	15 G6
Station Rd, Lower Weston BA1	8 D2
Steway La BA1	7 E1
Stirtingale Av BA2	9 E5
Stirtingale Rd BA2	8 D6
Stoke Mead BA3	15 E4
Stonefield Cl BA15	17 G4
Stonehouse Cl BA2	14 A1
Stonehouse La BA2	10 A6
Stoneleigh Ct BA1	5 H4
Stratton Rd BS31	18 B1
Stuart Pl BA2	9 E3
Sulis Manor Rd BA2	13 E3
Summer La BA2	14 A1
Summerfield Rd BA1	5 H5
Summerfield Ter BA1	5 H5
Summerhill Rd BA1	5 E5
Summerlays Ct BA2	10 A3
Summerlays Pl*, Pulteney Rd BA2	10 A3
Sunnybank BA2	10 A5
Sunnyside Gdns BA3	19 B2
Sunnyside Vw BA2	20 B3
Sunnyvale BA3	19 A4
Sunset Cl BA2	20 C3
Sutton St BA2	10 A1
Swainswick Gdns BA1	6 B4
Swainswick La BA1	6 B1
Swallow St BA1	3 C4
Sydenham Bldgs BA2	9 F3
Sydenham Rd BA2	9 F3
Sydenham Ter BA2	14 B1
Sydney Bldgs BA2	10 A3
Sydney Mews BA2	10 A2
Sydney Pl BA2	10 A1
Sydney Rd BA2	10 A1
Sydney Wharf BA2	10 A2
Symes Pk BA1	4 C4
Tadwick La BA1	6 A1
Tanners Walk BA2	8 A3
Taylors Row BA15	17 F3
Teddington Cl BA2	8 D4
Tennyson Pl BA2	9 G5
Tennyson Rd BA1	9 E1
Terrace Walk BA1	3 C4
The Avenue, Claverton BA2	10 D3
The Avenue, Combe Down BA2	14 A1
The Avenue, Timsbury BA3	19 B2
The Barton BA2	18 A4
The Batch, Bath BA1	7 E3
The Batch, Bristol BS31	18 C1
The Beeches BA2	13 E1
The Brow, Combe Down BA2	14 B1
The Brow, Twerton BA2	8 C3
The Chestertons BA2	7 E6
The Circle BA2	8 C5
The Circus BA1	3 A1
The Corridor BA1	3 C3
The Croft, Bath BA2	14 D2
The Croft, Bradford-on-Avon BA15	16 C6
The Daglands BA3	19 E4
The Elms, Bath BA1	6 B4
The Elms, Bradford-on-Avon BA15	17 E1
The Firs, Combe Down BA2	14 A1
The Firs, Limpley Stoke BA3	15 F5
The Folly BS31	18 D3
The Glebe, Freshford BA3	15 F6
The Glebe, Timsbury BA3	19 B1
The Glen BS31	18 C3
The Grove BA1	4 D5
The Heritage BA3	19 E4
The Hill BA3	15 G6
The Hollow BA2	8 B5
The Laurels BA15	16 C6
The Linleys BA1	9 E1
The Macies BA1	4 C4
The Mall BA1	3 C5
The Maltings BA15	17 F4
The Maltings Ind Est BA1	**8 C2**
The Mead, Bath BA3	19 C2
The Mead, Bradford-on-Avon BA15	16 B2
The Mews BA1	4 B6
The Mill Ho BA15	17 G3
The Normans BA2	7 E5
The Old Batch BA15	17 E1
The Orchard, Combe Down BA2	14 A2
The Orchard, Corston BA2	18 B4
The Orchard, Freshford BA3	15 G6
The Oval BA2	9 E5
The Paddock BA2	18 B4
The Paddocks BA2	14 A2
The Pastures BA15	16 B6
The Ridge BA15	17 G2
The Ropewalk*, Newtown BA15	17 F3
The Shallows BS31	18 D1
The Shambles BA15	17 F2
The Square, Bath BA2	9 G3
The Square, Timsbury BA3	19 C2
The Tyning, Bathwick BA2	10 A4
The Tyning, Freshford BA3	15 F6
The Weal BA1	4 D4
The Wilderness BA15	17 F2
The Willow Falls BA1	6 D4
The Woodlands BA3	19 F1
Third Av BA2	9 E3
Thomas St BA1	5 H6
Thornbank Gdns BA2	3 A6
Thornbank Pl BA2	9 G3
Titan Barrow BA1	7 H4
Toll Bridge Rd BA1	6 D4
Tory BA15	17 E3
Tory Pl BA15	17 E3
Trafalgar Rd BA1	4 D5
Treenwood Ind Est BA15	**17 F5**
Trenchard Rd BS31	18 B2
Triangle East BA2	9 E3
Triangle North BA2	9 E3
Triangle West BA2	9 E3
Trim Bri BA1	3 B3
Trim St BA1	3 B3
Trinity Cl BA1	3 A4
Trinity Rd BA2	10 A6
Trinity St BA1	3 A4
Trollopes Hill BA2	15 E1
Trossachs Dr BA2	6 B6
Trowbridge Rd BA15	17 F3
Tucking Mill La BA2	14 C3
Tunley Hill BA3	19 F2
Tunley Rd BA2	12 A5
Twerton Farm Cl BA2	8 C3
Tyning End BA2	10 A3
Tyning La BA1	6 A5
Tyning Pl BA2	14 B1
Tyning Rd, Bathampton BA2	7 E5
Tyning Rd, Bradford-on-Avon BA15	16 B2
Tyning Rd, Bristol BS31	18 C3
Tyning Rd, Combe Down BA2	14 B1
Tyning Rd, Peasedown St John BA2	20 C3
Tyning Ter BA1	6 A5
Tynings Way BA15	16 B6
Ullswater Dr BA1	5 H4
Under Knoll BA2	20 D1
Underleaf Way BA2	20 C3
Union Pass BA1	3 C3
Union St BA1	3 C3
Union Ter BA2	3 B6
Uphill Dr BA1	5 H4
Uplands Cl BA3	15 E4
Uplands Dr BS31	18 C3
Uplands Rd BS31	18 C3
Upper Bloomfield Rd BA2	13 E2
Upper Borough Walls BA1	3 B3
Upper Bristol Rd BA1	9 E2
Upper Camden Pl BA1	5 H6
Upper Church St BA1	9 G1
Upper East Hayes BA1	6 A6
Upper Furlong BA3	19 B1
Upper Hedgemead Rd BA1	9 H1
Upper Lambridge St BA1	6 B5
Upper Lansdown Mews BA1	5 G6
Upper Mill BA15	17 G3
Upper Oldfield Pk BA2	9 F3
Upper Regents Pk BA15	17 F3
Upper Westwood BA15	16 A6
Vale View Pl BA1	6 A5
Vale View Ter BA1	7 E3
Valley View Cl BA1	6 A4
Valley View Rd BA1	6 A4
Van Diemens La BA1	5 G4
Vane St BA2	10 A2
Vellore La BA2	10 A2
Vernham Gro BA2	13 E1
Vernon Cl BS31	18 A2
Vernon Pk BA2	9 E2
Vernon Ter BA2	9 E2
Vernslade BA1	4 C4
Vicarage Gdns BA2	20 B2
Victoria Bldgs BA2	9 F2
Victoria Bridge Ct BA2	9 F2
Victoria Bridge Rd BA2	9 F2
Victoria Cl BA2	8 D4
Victoria Cotts BA2	13 G4
Victoria Gdns BA1	6 D3
Victoria Ho BA1	5 E6
Victoria Pk Bsns Centre BA1	**9 E1**
Victoria Pl BA2	14 B1
Victoria Pl*, St Saviours Rd BA1	6 B5
Victoria Rd, Bath BA2	9 E3
Victoria Rd, Bristol BS31	18 B2
Victoria Ter BA2	9 E3
Victory Flds BA15	17 F4
Vine Cotts BA15	17 E2
Vineyards BA1	3 C1
Walcot Bldgs*, London Rd BA1	5 H6
Walcot Gate BA1	9 H1
Walcot Loop Rd BA1	3 C2
Walcot Par BA1	5 H6
Walcot St BA1	3 C1
Walcot Ter BA1	5 H6
Waldegrave Rd BA1	5 F5
Wallace Rd BA1	6 A5
Walmesley Ter*, Snow Hill BA1	6 A6
Walnut Dr BA2	9 F3
Waltining La BA2	18 D5
Walwyn Cl BA2	8 B2
Wansdyke Bsns Centre BA2	**9 E4**
Wansdyke Rd BA2	13 E1
Warleigh Dr BA1	7 F3
Warleigh La BA1	7 G6
Warleigh Rd BA1	11 G1
Warminster Rd, Bathwick BA2	10 B1
Warminster Rd, Limpley Stoke BA3	15 E6
Warwick Rd BA1	9 E3
Warwick Villas BA2	9 E3
Washpool La BA2	8 B6
Waterhouse La BA3	15 E2
Waterloo Bldgs BA2	8 C3
Watermead Cl BA1	3 A4
Watery La BA2	8 C3
Wayfield Gdns BA1	7 E2
Weal Ter BA1	4 D4
Weatherly Av BA2	13 E1
Wedgwood Rd BA2	8 B3
Wedmore Pk BA2	8 C5
Wedmore Rd BS31	18 B1
Weekesley La BA3	19 C4
Weir Pl BA15	17 F3
Weirside Mill BA15	17 G3
Wellington Bldgs BA1	4 D5
Wellow La BA2	20 A3
Wellow Mead BA2	20 A3
Wellow Tyning BA2	20 C3
Wellowcroft BA2	20 B3
Wells Rd, Bath BA2	3 A6
Wells Rd, Corston BA2	8 A5
Wellsway BA2	9 G4
Wellsway Pk BA2	13 F3
West Av BA2	9 E3
West Cl BA2	8 B4
West Lea Rd BA1	4 C6
West View Orchard BA3	15 G6
West View Rd BA1	7 F3
Westbrook Pk BA1	4 C4
Westbury Vw BA2	20 D2
Westerleigh Rd BA2	14 A1
Westfield BA15	17 E2
Westfield Cl BA2	9 F5
Westfield Pk BA1	8 B1
Westfield Pk South BA1	8 B1
Westgate Bldgs BA1	3 B4
Westgate St BA1	3 B4
Westhall Rd BA1	9 E1
Westmead Gdns BA1	4 C4
Westmoreland Dr*, Westmoreland St BA2	9 F3
Westmoreland Rd BA2	9 G3
Westmoreland Station Rd BA2	9 F3
Weston Farm La BA1	4 D3
Weston La BA1	4 D5
Weston Lock Retail Pk BA2	**8 D2**
Weston Park Ct BA1	5 E5
Weston Pk BA1	5 E6
Weston Pk East BA1	5 E6
Weston Pk West BA1	5 E6
Weston Rd BA1	5 E6
Westwood Rd BA15	16 D6
Westwood Vw BA2	13 E2
Westwoods BA1	7 F3
Weymouth St BA1	6 A6
White Horse Rd BA15	16 B2
White Ox Mead La BA2	20 D1
Whitebrook La BA2	20 A2
Whitefield Cl BA1	7 G2
Whiteheads La BA15	17 F2
Whitemore Ct BA1	7 E2
Whiteway Av BA2	8 C6
Whiteway Rd BA2	8 B6
Whitewells Rd BA1	5 H4
Wick House Cl BS31	18 B1
Wick La BA3	19 F4
Widbrook Hill BA15	17 H6
Widbrook Vw BA15	17 H4
Widcombe Cres BA2	10 A4
Widcombe Hill BA2	10 A3
Widcombe Ter BA2	10 A4
William St BA2	3 D2
Williamstowe BA2	14 B1
Willow Cl BA2	13 F2
Willow Grn BA2	9 F5
Wiltshire Way BA1	5 H4
Winchester Rd BA2	9 F3
Windrush Cl BA2	8 B4
Windsor Bridge Rd BA2	9 E2
Windsor Villas BA1	9 E2
Windy Ridge BA15	16 B6
Wine St, Bath BA1	3 C5
Wine St, Bradford-on-Avon BA15	17 E2
Wine Street Ter BA15	17 F3
Winifreds La BA1	5 F6
Winsley Hill BA3	15 F4
Winsley Rd BA15	16 C2
Witney Cl BS31	18 B2
Wood St, Bath BA1	3 B3
Wood St, Bath BA2	3 B4
Woodbine Pl*, Hatfield Bldgs BA2	10 A3
Woodhouse Rd BA2	8 B2
Woodland Gro BA2	13 F4
Woodlands Dr BA3	15 F4
Woodlands Pk BA1	5 H4
Woods Hill BA3	15 E4
Woolley Cl BA15	17 G2
Woolley Dr BA15	17 G2
Woolley Grn BA15	17 H1
Woolley La BA1	5 G1
Woolley St BA15	17 F2
Woolley Ter BA15	17 G2
Worcester Bldgs BA1	6 A5
Worcester Cl BA2	20 C3
Worcester Ct BA1	6 A5
Worcester Pk BA1	6 A5
Worcester Pl BA1	6 A5
Worcester Ter BA1	6 A6
Worcester Villas BA1	6 A5
Yomede Pk BA1	8 C1
York Bldgs BA1	3 B2
York Pl BA1	6 A6
York St BA1	3 C4